ELIZABETHAN DRAGONFLIES

THE POEMS OF
MIKE READ

ISBN NO. 1 871406 06 4

Ⓟ1988 Published by Goodyer Associates Ltd.
3rd Floor, 25 Market Place, Nuneaton, Warwickshire CV11 4EG.

Printed and bound in Great Britain by
View Publications (Bristol) Ltd.

ELIZABETHAN DRAGONFLIES

THE POEMS OF
MIKE READ

Cover and illustrations by
Melissa Gaye Goodyer

GOODYER ASSOCIATES

To the dreamers and romantics of this world

CONTENTS

Elizabethan Dragonflies 1

Return To Effingham 2

Dreaming 3

Midsummer's Day 1986 7

The Sunday Round 8

Rain - Mayfair and Knightsbridge 10

Oilbury 11

Above St Enodoc 12

Bottling Out 14

The Man With A Guitar - 1914 15

Suffolk Borders 16

World Without End 17

The Mad Hatter's Regatta 18

'Doubles' 19

Dripping Apples 21

Anchorites 22

Drinks - 7.30.. 23

Lands End 25

The Old Vicarage, Grantchester 26

Hurlingham Ball 31

Shimmering Armada 32

Rutland 33

Crossing the Tyne 34

Invergowrie 35

Under The Skylight 37

The Walkers 38

Middle Of The Day 40

Lytham St. Annes 41

Nothing 42

Daffodils 43

Kidderminster 44

Oblivious 45

William Hickey - 1933-1987 48

Centre Court Sonnet 49

Six O'Clock High 50

Sloth 52

Dreaming Spires 53

Polesden Lacey 55

Goodbye Old Friends 56

Newquay 58

The Calling 59

Upon Westminster Bridge - 4 March, 1987 60

West Bexington-on-Sea 61

The Bells of Cherbourg 62

From the Shores of Far Loch Lomond 63

There's A House On Rock Of Ages 64

Prayer 68

ELIZABETHAN DRAGONFLIES

I can't believe that all I see is mine.
The Chinese wing-nut walnut and the gorse,
The Swedish whitebeam poplar and the pine,
The Holden Brook that's just begun its course,
The twisting paths where once Edwardian feet
Investigated labyrinths of green.
Victorian drabness distant and effete
Washed away by landscape and machine.
The Jekyll-haunted gardens now are mine.
I walk at will down long untrodden tracks
Which halt the hands on the waistcoat watch of time.
Still frozen here the long-dead Georgian hacks.
Elizabethan dragonflies reverse,
I'll ride with you for better or worse.

RETURN TO EFFINGHAM

Return to Effingham cheap awayday
Countryside for city folk;
Winter, Easter, Whitsun, May-day,
Streaming out like runny yolk.

Effingham Station "please alight for
Gallows grave and Brick Kiln Copse,
Old Oak Common, Bushy Thicket -
Horsley, Clandon, next two stops."

British Railway Southern Region,
Branch line trade no 125's;
Running time complaints are legion,
Grumbling home to evening lives.

The winds of winter tug at bowler,
Wrench at glove, at bag and scarf;
Surrey station snows turn polar,
Cut the daylight hours in half.

Effingham village cats eyes twinkling
In the street lamp's sodium glare;
December snow is dusting, sprinkling
Festive feelings everywhere.

DREAMING

Dreaming past the fields of dead caravans
And half-built breeze-block garages,
Patched up with the still damp Sunday morning cement
Of a North Crewe Seventh-Day Adventist.
Sliding by the hives of sleeping Diesels
And empty red and yellow Royal Mail coaches;
Peeping out from a hoarding shrieking
Emirate promises of 'Dubai in Two Sheiks'.

Ranks of Ragwort devouring Vauxhall Wyverns,
Yawning standard Vanguards, Ford Cortinas -
Slowly strangled by advanced flora.
Watched by fresians from knee-high football field
And on to where the factories are resting.
'Universal grinding wheels' lies dormant,
'Prefabrication presswork' snugly torpid,
On this quiescent Staffordshire Sabbath Day

Snaking into black-bricked Stafford station.
Already there the blue 'Earl Marischal'
Adorned with undying eternal devotion,
Scratched in the thin layer of grime
Adolescent hieroglyphics
That the Midland deciphers as 'Lynn loves Gaz'.
A proclamation that is carried
Through the electrified afternoon to Euston.

Screened by Bogie Bolsters of grey stone chips
The custodians of the allotments,
Paper and plastic homemade scarecrows,
Flap and crack and terrify the carrion,
Baffled by the blue-striped Tesco bags
As they wheel and watch the lettuce grow.
Four placid, tolerant, and weather-worn horses
Hide from flies under the remains of an elm.

All along the Trent and Mersey canal
Intermittent bursts of yellow gorse flash out,
As June campers gaze at inclement weather
Through translucent polythene windows,
And luckless anglers bait the stream
With maggot, cheese and worms and bread.
A world of swirling mystery and reeds
65 miles away from Liverpool Lime Street.

Dreaming past the nine squat cooling towers,
Belching and spewing legionnella
On to the black-faced sheep-littered meadows
And the seven league boots of the giant striding pylons
Calling 'come to the new church and worship Electricity.'
Give thanks to Telecom and the B.B.C.
Strew their paths with underground cables,
And pray to megahertz with frequency.

Then the awesome stark spires of Lichfield.
Back to reality with dark flashing blade
Pressing with insistent urging fingers;
Jutting a thought-provoking skywards warning
And reminding me of you with your real faith,
And All-consuming Waugh-like enthusiasm,
Conviction running through you end to end,
Like a freshly lettered stick of Roman rock.

Whilst far to the South and the plains of Salisbury
Hippies attempt to pursue their line of belief,
Carrying through their faith and hopes
To the very foothills of the ancient Druid Circle.
Whether founded or misguided, a seemingly simple mission
Hampered only by desperate waves of Christians,
Atheists and Agnostics and others,
Clad as one in the battle-dress of the blue lamp.

Corrugated Trent valley factories
Thinly disguised by lamentable willows,
Savaged and ravaged, the stunted cypress screen
Ill-advisedly set in life-giving concrete.
Multi-coloured climbing frames and swings;
The official healthy council place to play.
Under several coats of grudging goodwill
Their still-pristine condition a testimony to their use.

Sliding on a shaft of sharp afternoon sun
Into the brightly scaffolded Rugby,
Where William Webb Ellis first ran with the ball,
And where Tom Brown scurried from the long shadows of Flashman;
Where Rupert Brooke with 'ball in hand and book in pocket'
Turned out for XI and the XV.
And the influence of Thomas Arnold
Lingers in long corridors of time.

Hastily discarded Sunday bicycles,
Wheels still spinning, by the long-stop boundary;
Spokes flashing in the weakening evening sun
As the first change bowler bouncing to the crease
Delivers an unplayable leg break to the tail,
Rapidly falling amidst flying balls.
One by one the quick return to the Pavilion,
Grim faced, with former fortitude erased.

Dreaming past the wide horse-chestnuts
Under the low oppressive heavens,
Reaching down to spired Harrow.
Draped like nets around the steeple,
Veils of melancholy rain clouds
Close over the Betjemanian hilltop,
Over you and your denomination,
Back on Liverpool's Lime Street Station.

MIDSUMMER'S DAY 1986

Midsummer's day on court at Badminton,
All keen to win the match against the breeze,
With six feet four of Bunter trying to cope
With cheering hounds and wild applauding trees.
Two hours from tea and two 'til early dinner,
The first set now a clear six games to three,
The next 6-4, the third 4-6 to them.
A victory for Bunter and for me.
The sweatsoaked whites still sticking to our backs,
Re-living every shot, along the paths,
As Gloucestershire wrapped summer round our legs,
While in the distance lapped the running baths.

THE SUNDAY ROUND

Incessant the rain on the first
Rhododendrons.
Incessant the rain on
Observer and Times.
But buoyant, the paperboy
Blinks from his pac-a-mac,
Like a beacon of light on a
Sunday he shines.

Check the results in the dry
Of the privet hedge,
Did Bury beat Brentford? -
Oh, only a draw.
With sports pages damp, it
Slides through the letter-box
Into the jaws of the dog on
The floor.

The paperboy's bane - the
Thick colour supplement,
Section of arts and weekly
Review,
Have to go through a gap
That was built just for letters -
Do I fold them in four, or in
Three, or in two?

Canvas bag empty, its back
To the paper shop,
Spray from the bicycle,
Chain that still sticks.
A triumphant return, its the
prodigal paperboy,
Holding his hand out for
19/6d.

RAIN - MAYFAIR AND KNIGHTSBRIDGE

The Regent Street shop-front excitement gone
And potted bay trees like winter-weathered doormen,
Green-liveried, grace each side of the supper club,
Inhaling double-breasted business men
From the vacuum between office and suburbs.
The gaping wounds of washed out Berkeley Square,
Where the decadent Astor was torn from its roots
Are scaffolded, sculpted, boarded, bucketed,
Laddered, quagmired, nightingale-free.
The Inn on the Park and Intercontinental nestle
Shoulder to shoulder at the end of Park Lane,
Where the rain and wind wrenches at the Union
And Maple Leaf flags, sodden and wind-wrapped,
Flapped till exhausted around the evening standards.
Hyde Park Corner, obsidian chariot,
Its fire quenched and jet black silhouetted against
The rough, buff backdrop of buffeting clouds.
Dead skips lie in Grosvenor Crescent and Belgrave Square,
Brim full of the laughter of yesterday's homes.
Coved cornices ripped from their corners and ceilings,
Balustrades, bannisters, banished for good.
Created with love by Edwardians, Georgians,
Chernobyl rain slowly drowning them all.
Swish Sloane Street mini-coach unloads pretty people
Who splash through the puddles to the Holiday Inn,
With grime-spattered court shoes, turn-ups, coat-tails,
Cocktail-bound, ball-bound in the happiness dome.
The court of King Harrod with illuminated spectred
Necklace strings, looms like a vast Titanic,
Foundering in the sheets of the gusting rain
To the distant sounds of Knightsbridge March.

OILBURY

Dad, may we see the nodding donkeys?
Do lets go to Newlands corner -
I've heard it said that long ago
There once was flora here and fauna.

Dad, may we see the pretty ribbons
Of entwining access roads,
Where once there lived, though I'm not certain,
Rabbits, Badgers, Foxes, Toads?

Dad, may we go one summer evening
When the noise is at it's height,
To breathe in deep those fumes of sulphur
Yellowing the August light?

Dad, is it true they once played cricket
On this thousand acre site?
And was the Tillingbourne a river
Long before they had it piped?

Dad, may we see the drilling derrick
And the cesspool drainage too?
Dad do tell me of the time
When Albury met its Waterloo.

ABOVE ST ENODOC

They came in a steady trickle,
Over the dunes, over the golf course,
Under the abrupt rise of Brea Hill
And with sudden reverence through the lych gate.
'Why here it is right by the entrance!
Isn't it funny it doesn't say 'Poet'
It doesn't say 'Sir' and he was wasn't he?
Well that's it then - there it is,
Unless you want a souvenir shot.
Will the letters show up alright?
Take another in case the first doesn't come out.
Point to it then! Smile - smile!'
No chance of excusing yourself with a
'Would you mind, I'd rather not'
No welcoming smile, no 'please', no 'thank you'.
Mute party to a thousand clicking Kodaks,
'I stood next to him you know - here's the proof!'
The trickle ran steadily on
Through the blue but windy August,
Following the white stones there and back
For their three or four minutes with you -
A pilgrimage sans conversation.
No! 'Would you like some tea - the kettle's on?'
No! 'Did you find the path too steep?'
Just silent memories neatly trimmed,
Second hand and, as an afterthought,
'Oh here's his mother too - they must have liked it here.
Once covered by sand the pamphlet says.
Do you think that it could be again?'
'Not in our lifetime,' answered a northern voice,
Hoisting up his ill-fitting trousers,
Sniffing and tucking in his T-shirt.

I was overcome by that dreadfully selfish feeling -
Of not wanting to share the moment with others
Or wanting to stay until early evening,
When the trickle had dried for the day
And have a private conversation.
'I'm sure I understand you more than most.'
I retired a few yards uphill to the 14th tee,
Discovered that 355 yards is 325 metres
And wrote this between the ragwort and the dandelions,
Watching the steady trickle come and go.

BOTTLING OUT

I've been Harris'd, I've been Marplan'd,
I've been Gallop'd, I've been Mori'd,
Had a thousand little leaflets through the door;
With photographs of candidates
From the feckless to the florid,
Lying with the bills upon the floor.

I've been Thatcher'd, I've been Kinnock'd,
I've been Owen'd, I've been Steele'd,
I've been Monster Raving Loony partied too;
I've had Hills and Ladbrook's offer me
Just '4-1 the field',
Except the Tories 'on at 9-2'.

I've been BBC'd and ITV'd,
Been Channel Four'd and cabled,
From Penzance to Orkneys, Rhyl to Tyne and Wear;
I've heard motions carried, motions vetoed,
Motions passed and tabled,
I've a notion they're all verbal diarrhoea.

I've been Sun'd and I've been Mirror'd,
Been Express'd and I've been Mail'd,
Guardian'd, Times'd and Telegraph'd till I'm lost;
But of each party manifesto
There is one that has not failed,
So the 'bring a bottle party' gets my cross.

THE MAN WITH A GUITAR - 1914

Monkey in the paintbox, feline on the keyboards,
Born of the Impressionists
And oil-dappled seaboards.

Paris, Salon d'Automme, ex-disciple of the Fauves,
Paints the door into the century
With pinks and blues and mauves.

Temper in the palette, cat-a-natural-lystic,
Push out the Cubist longboats here,
Our flags anomalistic.

Jigsaw on the easel, puzzle on the canvas.
A tie, an eye, a part of mouth,
Formless, footless, handless.

Green in strip and stripe shape, shades to rival nature
In the varying intensity
Of Braques own colorature.

Genius of deception and blindly overrated
Sombre painters of the Paris school,
Verbally berated.

Cezanne on the shoulder - Picasso's mind eclectic
And Les Desmoiselles d'Avignon
See nature geometric.

SUFFOLK BORDERS

Cavendish, Clare and Stoke-by-Clare,
Strung out in mid-November air.
Medieval sun drowns winter farms
As limbless windmills dwarf the barns.
Like black confetti on the run,
Some silent birds chase winter sun.
Cambridgeshire, Suffolk and Essex entwine
'Round Stour-ribboned borders of morning time.

WORLD WITHOUT END

From the world of St. George Street, Sothebys, sandwich bars,
Single and mingling with Cowdray Park crowds,
Bond Street excursions for Liberty headscarves,
A vista of youth with no gathering clouds.

From the world of the Whirlybird, Sea-King, Sikorsky,
Grand naval dockyard - the Empire's old door.
Ill-furnished cabins with locker-room pin-ups
Companions and oceans still there to explore.

The pukka-mixed cocktail, marquees on the polo lawns.
Chukka-chased ponies and hampers from home
Is the place to re-kindle a dwindling relationship -
Someone you have seen all your life though not known.

Into the world where the media makes you
And shakes the foundations of fashions and friends,
The TV and press men possess and molest you,
Pursuing relentlessly - world without end.

The yellow brick road does not go on forever.
To all flowers of Chelsea comes Autumn's chill breath.
Your name etched forever in Britain's first family,
In marriage, in motherhood, life and in death.

THE MAD HATTER'S REGATTA

The carnival air of the Henley Regatta,
Crackling like static for those in mid-stream.
See the Englishman play, he's as mad as a hatter,
For that matter so is the rest of the team.

Attempts at the Beatles drift over the water,
Well out of their depth and well out of their key.
'Ticket to Ride' and 'Lady Madonna'
Like 'ducks and drakes' flat stones come skimming to me.

Shades of the Test Match take place after supper
As one would-be Botham with champagne-cork leap,
Let's fly from the stern with a five metre yorker,
For the oar-toting batsman to drive to the deep.

Another ball - courtesy Moet et Chandon's
Expended with force and he just gets a touch.
All the Gattings and Gowers in Regatta-striped blazers
Appeal as it lands in the keeper's safe clutch.

The sea of umbrellas are fast disappearing,
The earlier clouds roll to Reading and Slough.
In time for the fireworks, the Henley sky's clearing,
In my head is the first line of 'Disney Girls' now.

Hundreds of small craft decks weighed down under
The annual punters, whose heaven-bent heads
Follow each rocket with an eight year old's wonder
And the 'ooh's' and the 'aah's' for the blues and the reds.

Punts brimming full of eccentrics straw-boatered,
Patrician of face are their feminine friends
Who came here by train, maybe cycled or motored,
To be part of this mad carousel on the Thames.

'DOUBLES'

The newly whitewashed wood pavilion
Dumbly watching dreary doubles,
Flanked by fast-growing cypress trees
That remind me of the back of 'Rubber Soul!'
Where, in the bottom left-hand corner,
Naive yet wise, the face of Lennon
Poses by conifer from 'Kenwood',
Though it might not have been St. George's Hill,
'In my life' was wonderful -
Why couldn't I have written something
That came within a mile of that?
'Do concentrate' said voices from the court.

What's the score - oh 30 - 40,
I quite lost count through screaming children
Shrieking over squeaking swings,
Parental palpitations running fast
Pitched so low they don't quite register,
Monosyllabic juveniles
Queue for lollies and '99's',
In cheap blue jeans from British Home Store shops
And lopping off the lowest branches,
The Birds Eye lorry with deliveries
Scrapes park-like trees with cold disinterest,
Once planted by now long-dead local mayors.

What's that now, deuce or advantage?
Happy mud-caked cocker spaniel
Trailing after hopeful children,
Off to dredge the paddling pool with nets.
Perhaps a mackerel in the shallows,
Wallowing in corporation water,
Imaginary catch in plastic bucket.
I can't believe we've lost that set already.
Dark-haired girl like Mona Lisa,
Mystery lightening her pretty face,
All along the wire netting ...
Missed it! Our opponents served an ace!

Pottering local wanders slowly.
Are his thoughts in '86
Or back among his pre-war boyhood,
When he would have joined us for a 'four'?
The heavens darken and he wonders,
'Will I get home before it rains?
Shrinking skin I have already,
I'd hate my only suit to do the same.'
Another set! I don't believe it!
Prawn sandwiches I'd like for lunch.
Gastronomic consolation.
Two sets down and playing 'the best of five'.

DRIPPING APPLES

The sturdiest tree that leans by brambled copse
Is dripping apples, August green and firm,
Not too unripe to feed the fledgling crops,
Not too unripe for hovering wasp or worm.
Fulfilled, the blossomed promise of the spring;
No April frost to seize it in its prime.
Soon choirs at harvest festival will sing
'The crops grow tall' at apple-ripening time
And that's because God comes down in the rain
And in the warmth of long hot afternoons,
I sit beneath the tree and pick refrains;
In dappled sun I shape them into tunes.

ANCHORITES

How would Gilbert Holl and Boehm, those local academicians,
Portray today on canvas, Shere's latest propositions?
In R.A. hands the Tillingbourne is usually compelling,
But the view's obscured by garages and red brick modern dwellings.
And in several years if all goes well under Labour or the Tories,
The Church could be quite possibly, dwarfed by multi-storeys.
While anaesthetized and shrink-wrapped on the fire station site,
An attractive supermarket with glowing neon lights.

And where the forge stood now there stands a brand new discotheque,
Which should rile the fuddy-duddys who want to counter check
The construction traffic's wheels of progress in every Surrey village.
With protective helmets - Viking style - they demolish, rape and pillage.
To change the character of Shere would seem most injudicious.
Domesday island quite untouched till developers avaricious,
Take us for 'Rural Rides' with a difference - the thin end of the wedge,
They'll start at the heart and systematically bulldoze to the edge.

Applications for development could swamp the borough council.
New shops would root like mares-tail, estates would spread like
groundsel.
They'd do well to heed the story of the Anchoress of Shere:
Incarcerated in her cell for year on lonely year,
Her contact with the world outside from small and darkened room,
Was an aperture, through which came food and light into the gloom.
I hear they're building more of these - hurry! Acquire the rights,
So that Shere men of the future may all be Anchorites.

DRINKS - 7.30

Tell me, Captain, how is Pirbright?
Pinot Grigio -wise that is -
Tell me, through the roasted peanuts,
Of your sojourn in Cadiz.
Bombard my Frascati'd grey cells
With your dulcet drill square drone.
Fascinate me with your memoirs,
Now you're almost fully grown.

Thrill me with your stock exchanges
While I count your greying hairs.
Live again those indices,
Please peddle me your pin-striped wares.
Drown me in your Veuve du Vernay,
Intrigue me with your gilt-edged tongue.
Jab it home with index finger,
Spill F.T. on everyone.

Instruct me on negotiations
In vendor, vendee, ventus, vein.
Take me through exchange of contracts,
Entangle me in lengthy chain,
Until completion drains the Vouvray.
Top up now while buoyancy lasts,
Ten per cent is semi-listening,
Watching you leave little casts.

You must have a head for figures,
Eyes both have at least I see,
And margin running down your jacket
Inevitably figure free.
Chartreuse accountant Old Carthusian,
Let your bottled audit flow.
Although you're sending little sines,
My mind is firmly in Escrow.

LANDS END

I stood like an ancient on England's arm,
The final survivor of Lyonesse.
The watery grave of lost Arthurian wraiths,
Swallowed by the surging waves and less
Than twenty miles to the west hide the isles.
Samson, Tresco, Martin's, Mary's, Bryher,
And further south lurks Agnes in the Mist,
Which seems on summer nights to catch on fire.

THE OLD VICARAGE, GRANTCHESTER

(Cafe des Bleus, London, October 1986)

Just now October sun grows cold
And bathes the house in Autumn gold
Where Rupert Brooke's long shadow falls
Once Rugby formed, on garden walls
Where asters soured by acid rain
Lay down and don't get up again
Oh there is sonnets echo through
From World War 1 to World War 2,
And on decades up 'till today
Keeping all the world at bay
From the vicarage at Grantchester -
My solitude where none can pester
Chide or chase - a placid island
Not factory hemmed in there, or pyloned.
Long hot summers by the river
now give way to spinal shiver
That runs down me ...
du lieber Gott!

Here am I, in Parliament and hot
And there a Radox bath awaits
Which often more than compensates
For long hard deputy chairman hours
With Norman Tebbit. And there some flowers
Linger in nearing winter sun
Like brightly blazing cummerbund,
Holding in the tales of summer,
On the boards like well-primed mummer.
And there the unrelenting press
Now trample the grass to muddy mess,
For as many headlines as they can handle
It's "Career in Ruins" or "Bizarre Scandal"
"Tory Boss Archer Pays Off Vice Girl"
And "Monica Coghlan Looked Such a Nice Girl".

Set up yet innocent - would I were
In Grantchester in Grantchester,
miles from Shepherd Market's lights
Shining on ladies of the night,
Who telephone and claim liaison.
Fleet Street or Kyrie Eleison
On this 14 month old Tory
Deputy Chairman who swallowed the story
Of Monica harassed by the press,
Sounding genuinely under duress.
Then before the mystery could be solved
It seemed I was inextricably involved,
When tape recordings and photographs
(Muck-rakers don't do things by halves),

Were Fleet Street touted by Aziz Kurtha,
Who no one seemed to think was worth a
Second glance or time of day ...
Foolish!... what else can I say?
This ex-presenter (Channel Four)
Has made me look a fool ... what for?
They can't explain his motivation
For strange ideas above his station,
Seemingly no political grievance
No grudges via our antecedents.
And being well-heeled, not financial,
Nor was it only circumstantial.
So presses roll before the dawn;
A million headlines gape and yawn
"It's now become a Matterhorn
Of honour for Margaret's favourite Faun".
To step down and resign my post,
Return to live with the Cambridge ghost
Of Rupert Brooke and write more sequels
To best selling novels like "First Among Equals".
Lord Mishcon cannot save my bacon
I've been baited, hooked and taken
To the cleaners - left in tangles
Wrung through incessant Fleet Street mangles.

God! I will pack and pray to Heaven
The traffic is light on the M 11,
And the east bound queues on mad north circular
Are all free flowing - not tubercular.
To Cambridgeshire my destination,
Sanctuary from speculation,
Pursued from Thameside penthouse suite
By papparazzi, pressmen, fleet
Of foot and street, in neat new Fiats,
Heading north towards St. Neots
Off to Royston fit to burst
To get to south east Cambridge first,
To barricade my very door
And fire questions by the score.

"If not guilty why then pay?
Can blackmailers really get away
With travesties of justice, such
As needing cash so very much,
That for an outlay of 10p
Donated to the S.T.D.
They ask someone they've never met
To somehow or another get
A grand or two to a destination...
Say, Platform 3, Victoria Station.
And the ideal thing remedially,
Is to use an intermediary.
So Michael Stackpoole meets the whore
With two grand "not a penny more"."
Grantchester, ah Grantchester,
Safe from all their questions there,
And spectres from the past they'll drag
Screaming into Sunday rag.
Pious as hell and yet corrupt,
They stand aside while their quarries erupt.
As the ashes, dead by one decade,
Are raked and sifted, sortied, recce'd,
Then given quite a prominent splash
"You know he owed half a million cash
When bankruptcy loomed in '74:"
I must get to Grantchester before
The howling mob from E.C.4.
Batter down the vicarage door.
On, you olive green Daimler two,
Not many miles now in front of you.
AH GOD! the car telephone's faint burr,
Could it be Mary from Grantchester,
Or one of the wild pursuing pack
Putting me on the Telecom rack.
Shepherd Market! how I hate that name,
Mayfair will never seem the same.
And since the so called revelation
I'll read tabloids with trepidation.
Inevitably as weeks go by
I guess some bright young spark will try

To write a Jeffrey Archer novel
Complete with scandal, blackmail, brothel,
And I'll be left to ponder on
Midsummer words by Oberon
"Ill met by moonlight proud Titania"
In Grantchester my Oceania.
Sleepless nights asking the Lord
About the home truths from a broad,
That there's some corner of a foreign kind
That will play forever on my mind.
Home! and the vicarage door keeps back
Each tidal wave of leech-like hack.
When three I wanted to be four,
When four, Prime Minister, but by sod's law
Stands the blackmailer at ten to three,
And is there money still for free?

HURLINGHAM BALL

On this most English of summer evenings,
March the band of the Coldstream Guards.
Out of the deepening river shadows,
In scarlet lines through the chimes of midnight,
Past the glinting hoops of Hurlingham,
Through the croquet lawns, the tunics -
Ranks of patriotic bandsmen
Bathed in the glow of low key floodlights.
Pageantry in all its glory,
Stirs our souls with Jingoistic
Melodies from twinkling guardsmen,
On this most English of summer evenings.

SHIMMERING ARMADA

Shimmering Armada of the South Mersey,
Flickering like giant industrial pleasure parks
With illuminated roller coasters,
Pumping gaseous waste into the Mersey skies.
Blotting out the majority of midnight
Stars overshadowed by the cast display strung
Between Ellesmere Port and Runcorn. With the
Gargantuan chemical playgrounds straddling
The polluted sweep before it rushes up,
Swirling, to Port Sunlight and Birkenhead,
Bearing ferries to Belfast, Dublin, Douglas.
Across the Liverpool Bay and on past
The yawning mouth of the River Dee.
Shimmering cities reflected in the skies,
In the water, in the mind and in the eyes,
Like Blackpool illuminations out of season,
Glistening like romantic ocean liner.
Unseeing mammoths in tusk-to-tail trek
Following blindly across a vast plain,
Stumbling naively into their own demise.

RUTLAND

Return to us our stone-built Rutland,
Seventeen down, the same across;
For now we stand knee-deep on upland
Barley'd wold and mourn our loss.
Surrender every golden summer,
Every sleepy afternoon;
Despatch this instant news with runner,
All will be delivered soon.

Return to us our ancient churches,
Fifty, and no two alike;
Taken, not by legal purchase -
Counties shuffled in the night.
Yield the quarries stony heartland
Rocks from Rutland's gaping wounds;
Pluck it from its new found outland,
Tell us it will happen soon.

Relinquish all your rights to Rutland;
Uppingham and Oakham towns,
Have Mercia on ancient upland,
Royal forests, sunlit downs;
Pastoral East Midland valleys,
Snickets, avenues and lanes;
Plundered now our roads and alleys,
Once defended from the Danes.

CROSSING THE TYNE

Lashing out at promiscuity,
Block capitalled doom-laden warnings
Scream at inter-city windows
Ads for Aids on council hoardings.

Balding gricers, lunchtime multi-
Ply like rosebay willowherb,
Rooted there since steam-pulled childhood,
Now in second, some in third.

Dragged back by intercom commercial
Extolling the virtues of travellers fare,
For once not wholly incoherent,
Nor metallically impaired.

Mackerel or cock-a-leekie,
Salmon from the Dee and Tay;
Caboc, Gaelic, Orkney cheeses,
Rhubarb tart the traditional way.

A gentle run through slender tariff
For diners and those who abstain,
He offered a prayer as we crossed the Tyne
And blessed the food in Jesus' name.

INVERGOWRIE

One time all the birds in Scotland
Seemed to sing in Invergowrie.
As the sun set on Victoria
Jute mill workers, frozen Lowry,
In suspended animation,
Permanently at their station,
New Edwardian elation
Bloomed at Invergowrie.

As zephyrs of romantic summer
Tied unseen bows round Invergowrie,
She would walk with spirits soaring.
When the August fields were flowering
unfettered, free of all direction,
Nurturing her deep affection,
Exaggerated recollections
Invaded Invergowrie.

Soon the chilling winds of winter,
Tightly binding Invergowrie,
Form a wall that none may enter.
Nonetheless, she watches hourly
From the grey stone institution,
Pride rejection substitution,
Her thoughts are scrambled with solutions
At dark-houred Invergowrie.

Kneeling in the private chapel
Here in free church Invergowrie,
Knuckles white and clenched in prayer,
For this is where she wants to marry.
Where is he now? In consternation
She cries with wretched desperation.
Despair provides the motivation
For death at Invergowrie.

Eighty summers, eighty winters,
Have come and gone at Invergowrie,
And on this carousel of seasons
She rides, till every February,
Searching still with soul tormented,
Suicidal, late lamented,
On the gallery where life was ended,
She appears at Invergowrie.

UNDER THE SKYLIGHT

Cans of combustible chemicals to coiffure crowning glory
Into a Henry Moore exhibit worthy of Kensington Gardens,
Or a prominent hanging in the capital's Tate Gallery,
Rub shoulders with handed-down opaque anachronistic scent bottles,
Which once swept grandmother through the perfumed 30's to Ritz suppers,
And rubbed necks with sharp angled art deco scent-spray, mirror and
 hairbrush.
Saved time and time again from destruction, they cling to the 80's,
Travelling through time from generation to generation.
The lifeless Goblin teasmade gathers dust of unwanted mornings.
The intended dauphin of slothful flat-dwellers heralds no new day,
But squats in useless symmetry gathering layers and layers,
Watched by Jim Stark, Jett Rink and Caleb Trask late of highway 466,
Just as they watch from a million bedroom walls, sullen and faded;
Frozen before 'The left-handed gun' in September 1955.
Beneath the crumpled continental quilt of last night's colourful dreams,
Two bears play hide and seek, vying for affection in the dark.
Which one will it be tonight? The one with the wisdom of two decades,
Loved, increasingly hairless, or the new, synthetic and sloganed,
As fresh as the square boxed Fine Fare tissues in subtle shades of autumn?
Dwindling daily under winter ailments and rain-pummelled skylight
All are material footprints of the journey before I knew her;
Pages of the unturnable book I opened some way through the plot.

THE WALKERS

Army surplus boots crush autumn
Browns, and branches drip unceasing,
Brushing deep-inhaling faces.
Sunday walkers, only leasing
Rural vistas for the weekend.
Only routes well-marked and pre-mapped;
Only paths and lanes well-trodden.
Balaclava hat and ski-wrapped
In what Greenland Eskimos call
Anoraqs, to keep November's
Second wind a mere statistic,
Beaufort bound - the gale surrenders.

Duffle-coated, too, the walkers.
All the men are wiry-bearded,
Bursting through their crowning glory
Wondering what the lunchtime beer did.
Girlfriends look the same but shorter,
Each without the beards and thinning;
All played chess from early schooldays
R - B4, mate, and winning.
Each and every sombre walker
Weaned on Tolkien's tales of Gollum,
Middle Earth and Rings and Hobbits,
Trudge in single file and solemn.

Dungeon versus Dragons experts,
Strung out over gorse logged greensand,
Rucksack backed and leaning windwards,
Coarse socks stretched up over jeans and
hands red-bitten by November.
Sacrificial limbs delivered
To the well-worn route by Audi,
Driven back by lily-livered
White suburban folk - non walkers.
'Who wants to commune with nature?'
Exercise is changing channels
Not subjection to denature.

From Surbiton, the hikers wholemeal
Blessed with wheatgerm, filled with cheese,
Topped with sliced organic beetroot,
Squashed-in napkins on their knees.
Swallowed with enthusiasm
Under nimbus jet-filled skyways,
Rounded off with russet apple.
Joining bridle-path and byways,
Volumes full of Clare and Hardy
Stored behind their bookish lenses;
Turning pages as they're walking
Through the woods of Smiths and Menzies.

Under alders troop the walkers,
Past the scaly beech trees peeling;
Through the arch of ancient yew trees,
To the lofty cypress ceilings.
On and on towards December
Over Wilton needled flooring,
Moisture on each hirsute jawline
Drenched in nature overawing.
Slowly twilight dims the walkers;
Into shapes of dusk, and blending
In with Disney skies of evening,
Plod the walkers, never ending.

MIDDLE OF THE DAY

Mornings are fresh, new and optimistic;
Mornings are hope, rebirth, awakening.
The time for plans, schemes, plotting the future;
For deciding - today will be the day.

Evenings are long, short and resignation;
Evenings are for reflection and musing.
The time for memoirs and taking stock;
For wondering if today will be the day.

But the middle of the day is bland, dull;
Going neither forwards nor looking back.
Existing in a strange uneasiness;
The morning's gone, the evening may not come.

LYTHAM ST. ANNES

This corner of the world's at peace it seems
As Lytham sunlight drowns the afternoon,
Invading every fairway, bunker, green
And spilling over every grassy dune.
From here and there a distant glinting shaft
As irons are wielded silently and straight.
Green, Gary, Martin, John and I all laughed,
Each holing out in ten or nine or eight.
Our four all running in - please overtake!
And while they did we'd sit and watch the planes,
Commanche shadows on the man-made lake,
Young pipers wasp-like dropping from their lanes.
In early summer haze we soldiered on
Till shadows of the afternoon grew long.

NOTHING

Miss you? I won't miss you.
There's been nothing there to miss.
We rarely held each other's hands
And hardly ever kissed.
You never spoke with any feeling
- I never asked you to.
The odd involuntary squeeze
And cuddle had to do.
When my lips tried to touch your lips
You'd turn your head away.
At night you'd always sleep alone
And even through the day
You'd distance me without a word
Ever being spoken.
And breaking up is meaningless -
There was nothing to be broken.
There were no words to describe it -
No ecstasy, grief or bliss.
Miss you? I won't miss you.
There's been nothing there to miss.

DAFFODILS

Everywhere a blaze of yellow
Nodding late round Clandon churchyard,
Like a thousand tallow candles,
Flickering and richly nurtured.

Drifts on rural Surrey verges,
Early April evening's highlight.
Just as the day with night-time merges
Luminous in gathering twilight.

Brightly coloured stars of springtime,
Fluted bells that stand in stillness,
Light the way like guiding torches,
Comforting, dispelling illness.

Scattering last strands of daylight
On the tired, the drawn, the weary.
Lining lanes throughout the village,
Lifting spirits feeling dreary.

KIDDERMINSTER

The sunny red-brick Kidderminster semis,
Cypress-tree'd and wrought-iron gated,
Thread their way along the Birmingham Road,
Infested by weaving schoolboy cyclists
With knotted football boots on handlebars,
Shouting in a monosyllabic code
Whilst speeding home 'no hands' to fish fingers
And beans gobbled while transfixed to T.V.

The crispish, mid-March, Kidderminster country,
Patchwork-quilted, criss-crossed by minor roads,
All carrying crawling distant Dinky toys
Through heavy leaded country club windows,
Accompanied by cocktail lounge piano,
Audible yet indistinct melodies,
Lazily jazzed up on the ivories
By fingers long bored, and numbed by the years.

Spongy yielding Kidderminster garden
Where scruffy blackbirds flap in last week's rain,
Circling clumps of magpie-haunted pampas
And lining all the early spring birches.
The drooping shingle-spanning tennis net
Hangs unwanted across the latticed court.
By the quince-fanned walls of the fruit garden
A mid-20's mock-tudor shadow falls.

OBLIVIOUS

Sony Walkman blotting out the world.
Oblivious to all but 'Tears for Fears',
The album that reminds her just of him
Still plays incessantly inside her head.
'Songs from the Big Chair', waiting at Earls Court
Through sliding doors and sliding doors again
And up the escalator to the street,
Past advertisements for ladies' corsets
And out of gusting tube-blown dry warm air
Into a late September Oxford Street,
Where plate glass windows full of Hush Puppies,
Slingbacks, stilettos, Victorian lace-ups
And furry winter wellingtons abound;
Where the suitcase sellers with cheaper wares
Foist quick sale perfumes, 'Brand names only, 'Sir,'
On discontented businessmen who hope
A two ounce bottle of 'pomme d'or' will help
To assist their flagging suburban love life.
The black-laced lingerie from Bond Street worked,
Until accused of 'being odd' that is,
And now takes a back seat in the top drawer,
Unable to be thrown away for fear
Of being found and laughed at by the dustman.
'This cheap bottle of scent should do the trick.'
Bumper to bumper orange-flagged taxis
Wink attractively, to over-laden
Ladies for Woking, Walton, Surbiton,
Wimbledon and all stations from Waterloo.
Warm autumnal clothing they can ill-afford,
Packed in the back of Hackney carriages,
Each in expensive glossy carrier bag
Advertising Selfridges, B.H.S.

Through the wide aisle of indiscreet telephones,
A plastic multi-domed Tower of Babel,
Symmetrical as ladies' hairdriers.
Screamed at by this week's tantalizing mags -
Woman's Own, Woman's Realm, Tatler and Time,
And the Evenings with teasing headlines, 'only
Twenty pence,' expensive for a crossword
That becomes increasingly difficult
With fellow travellers on your shoulder,
And homeward schoolboys. Sweet plastic orange
Invading the tightly packed corridor;
A corridor of new newspaper print,
Tobacco impregnated Terylene,
Mysterious well-travelled briefcases,
Grey, unshaven, dissatisfied faces;
Unsavoury men who seem much too close,
Whether by accident or by design;
Who brush their work-worn body against yours
Guilty father clutching peacemaking toys
In a vain attempt at compensating
For all those nights away in pub and bars,
Members clubs, restaurants and brasseries.
As Mr. Men lay dusty and unread
And cries of '<u>when</u> will he be home?' are drowned
By the opening theme of Eastenders
Now filtering through the half-ajar door,
To the Postman Pat wallpapered bedroom.
Porters, once upon a time there to help
Have ears and eyes that avert each query,
As they gaze into the middle distance
And mutter an incoherent reply.
Each station buffet, once the hub of life
So full of the smell of hot sausage rolls,
Where steaming cups of Bovril brought to life
The frozen, stiffened, ungloved winter hands,
Seem permanently closed, unpatronised,
Unwanted by the surging rush-hour tide.
Eventually to home and 'Russell Hobbs'
And granary toast spread thinly with Gold,
Eaten in front of Nicholas Witchall,

Sue Lawley, and those other purveyors
Of news - political, social and sport.
But the album that reminds her just of him
Still plays incessantly inside her head.

WILLIAM HICKEY - 1933-1987

From '30s to '80s,
From Driberg to Miller,
Collecting the crumbs from
Society tables;
Steering the blue-blooded
Beaverbrook tiller,
Through the sea of reality,
Fiction and fables.

CENTRE COURT SONNET

The Puddles on the Centre Court grow deep;
Oh where have all those
Laver summers gone?
Those lazy sun-filled
Newcombe afternoons -
With Kodes at South
London's Parthenon.
       Pre-tie break days that
Players understood.
When long sets ended 21-19.
When players shirts and
Socks were gleaming white,
Not cluttered by an advertiser's dream.
Somewhere beyond the golf-umbrella sea
Pace Lendl, Edberg, Becker, Mayotte, Cash.
       While fans still tolerant can only dream
Of the long hot days of
Smith and Arthur Ashe
The Centre Court has now
Become a lake,
And the only service here is
Tea and cake.

SIX O'CLOCK HIGH

Six o'clock high on a summer's evening,
Tucked in the folds of the Sussex Weald;
Saxon chimes dissect the stillness,
The village XI are in the field.

Six o'clock high in a Georgian August,
Blazing sky and blazing stone;
Here in Belloc's tumbled garden,
Renoir's young shepherd stands alone.

Six o'clock high and crammed in the box pews,
Men of the village and wives of the men;
Cobbett's riding through copse and clearing,
With Browning and Tennyson wielding the pen.

Six o'clock high and the swallows are diving,
The village resounds to industrious ring;
The thump of the hammers, the fire of the forges,
The New Model Army is fighting the King.

Six o'clock high and sweeping from Andred,
Comes Harold of Wessex with Kentish men,
To meet defeat from the Norman invaders,
The Lake of Blood flows on unstemmed.

Six o'clock high in Andred's Weald,
Around the world tree yggdrasil;
Saxon Ash tree gods of Asguard,
Woden god-father and Loke the ill.

Six o'clock high in redemption white,
The sixth-day Druid with a golden knife
Climbed the sacred temple of Oak,
To cut the all-healing plant of life.

Six o'clock high and an unborn stillness,
Casts deep oppression on this darkest age,
'Til I struggle with passion and fight for breath,
Racing through time from page to page.

Seven o'clock high on a summer's evening,
I'm back, I blink and look around;
Stumps are drawn and there the groundsman,
Drags the roller up and down.

SLOTH

They sow the sullen seeds of discontent
With eyes expressionless as processed data.
Fixed of glare, like dead men, only straighter,
With brows like furrowed fields of deepest Kent,
Are smiled upon by none save their Creator.
Take nothing now then naught to repay later,
Sealed within the world that they frequent,
Where glowering resentment curdles faith.
When up before the final court, on oath
Is brought to light each swung gratuity.
Turns living youth to shapeless formless wraith.
There grips the dock the undefended sloth -
As in life in perpetuity.

DREAMING SPIRES

Physically you're here, spiritually you're not.
An erratic pendulum swinging
More one way than the other.
Happy without the equilibrium
You walk past the hunting scenes,
Past the Atkinson East Anglian sepias,
Past the cellar entrance and through the front door
Into the world of Dreaming Spires.

Verbally you're here, mentally you're not.
A displaced person running
On automatic pilot, yet
Not unaware of your obliviousness,
You drift past poetry drafts,
Past the 'Betjeman musical' cassettes,
Past the entrance marked 'me' and through the garden
Into the world of Dreaming Spires.

Technically you're here, abstractly you're not.
An unhappy person listening
To a song dropped from the chart,
Overplayed to the point of tedium
But cherished still as you press 'replay'
Then press 'reject', having thought again.
Then 'pause' on a sudden impulse,
On 'hold' your world of Dreaming Spires.

By a narrow chance you're here, broadly speaking you're not.
An unhappy soul that's wandering
With complete and utter freedom,
To the outer regions of the tethered rope.
I saw the lost and haunted look,
I heard a hundred words unsaid,
As I delivered you to the very gates
Of your dungeon of Dreaming Spires.

When uncommitted you're here, when committed you're not.
An inmate that's escaping
From the ring road that engulfs you,
Like a tarmac moat around your life.
I've seen the fast and shuttered gate,
I've seen the audience blinds come down,
I've smelled the lure of the opium den,
Calling you back to your Dreaming Spires.

POLESDEN LACEY

Shades of Sheridan's Dublin shadows
Past the long walk's barbered yews,
Low cut lawns like manicured meadows
From 'Rivals', 'Critics' good reviews,

And on the croquet lawn, Diana -
Dieties play Ionian rules.
On summer days a large bandanna
Mops the brows of Kings and fools.

For weekend guests, the wicker hamper.
Off to Albury, Ockley, Shere.
Mrs. Greville loves to pamper
Playboys, Politicians, Peers.

Strike the gong, you old retainer
Strutting penguin -5 o'clock!
Queen Anne silver, Queen Anne strainer,
Chantilly doyleys, Meissen pot.

Past curtain calls, the Polesden mummer
Lies between four statuettes
Of Autumn, Winter, Spring and Summer,
At beck and call like four soubrettes.

GOODBYE OLD FRIENDS

Goodbye old friends.
Pre-dating all on Earth who walk,
Who procreate, who breathe and wither,
Having stood beside you knowing
You'd outlast their frail bodies.
Dappled in September sunlight,
Draped in falls of deep December,
Heavy with the green of summer,
Now mis-shapen, stunted, twisted -
Your time came too soon,
Annihilated by the armies.
Nature's forces all combining,
Wreaking havoc in the night with
Rain and wind like Gog and Magog,
Leaving trails of bleak destructions,
Chaos, holocaust and carnage,
Stacked as foul plague-ridden bodies,
Haphazard waiting for the tumbril.
And now they are gone.
Shallow-rooted Firs and Rowans;
Yews of Village green and Churchyard;
Oaks and scaly Silver Birch Woods;
Seasoned Holly's, catkined Alders,
Sycamores and white Laburnum;
Weeping Willows, leaning Poplars,
Speckled flaky Planes and Beeches,
Now lie scattered, limbless, bleeding,
To be strangled by ivy.
With leaves still green, the chainsaws whine,
While roots like molars torn from gums
Leaving gaping open unhealed wounds

Like battalions wrenched from trenches,
Re-shaping vistas, changing skies.
One hundred times the sap that rose
Will rise no more. Now gone forever,
Whistling branches, shade from seasons.
Goodbye old friends.

NEWQUAY

Racing lemming-like to the edge of the land
Astride pneumatic drill engines,
Bursting from air-conditioned coaches
Like a circus finale they come,
Tumbling and shouting
In a bouncing mass of gaudy colours,
Carrying their lives to the beach.
Inflatable boats, balls, buckets and armbands,
Scratching towels, windbreaks, flasks and cans,
Spaniels, labradors, poodles, mongrels,
Newspapers, magazines and Barbara Cartland novels.
A 'nice little spot' that the tar has spared
Not too far from the municipal toilets,
With their lichen-covered roof,
Bright blue drainpipes and pebble-dash walls.
Close by the plastic bins that scream 'litter',
Spewing last night's contents gently on to the pavement.
Just within earshot of the traffic lights
And the inconsistent 'bleep' 'bleep' 'bleep'
Of the 'you have 10 seconds to cross' signal.
For 10p a view of where you might have been
Were you not where you are.
Inconsistent in clothes, in style, in dress,
They run the gauntlet of offensive youth,
Bored and arrogant, treating any who pass
To a string of moronic expletives,
Those with different accent as aliens,
The prematurely bald as senile,
And obese as vile.

THE CALLING

Still runs the Ivel through Bedfordshire shallows,
Still the reflection of blue from the sky;
Edged with the greenness by nettles of April,
And tinged with an effortless waving goodbye.

Break from the mooring the flat-bottomed rowboat,
To dance to the tune of the piper of dawn;
For now is the hour of natures reveille,
With me as a witness the softest of thorns.

I testify all that I see is beginning,
I swear re-creation by any known force;
By even the strongest most indefatigable,
Far from the powers of all but the source.

Gladly I drift through the new revelations,
Observer and lover of all that I feel;
Crossing the canvas with deference, humility,
Ever intruder and never quite real.

Still guiding, the strong unseen hand of the river,
Still calling the sirens that beckon me on;
Just one more bend, just one more, just one more,
The search for the grail, for the home of the song.

The hope in the budding green flags on the birches,
Is surely a sign that this might be the way;
So I'll follow the good heart that never stops beating,
Past hollow and emptiness, on into May.

UPON WESTMINSTER BRIDGE - 4 MARCH, 1987

Earth now has many things to show more fair.
When the London that once caught Wordsworth's eye
In clarity, with no polluted sky;
Was dressed by architects when unaware.
Caught in the spotlight or sodium glare.
Flats, high-rise blocks, chimneys and factories vie
For the attention of the passer-by,
Who does not see and doesn't even care.
Never did the sun more sluggishly creep
West from the estuary and Tower Hill,
Weakly over ignominious heap.
The murky, tainted Thames still swirls and swills.
Dear God! The city's dying, not just asleep.
Description would defy the Wordsworth quill.

WEST BEXINGTON-ON-SEA

Perhaps there is a part of me,
Still at West Bexington-on-Sea.

Where the land slopes to the ocean,
Where the Lyme Bay breakers crash
In perpetual emotion;
Wave by wave my hopes are dashed.

I know there is a part of me,
Still at West Bexington-on-Sea.

Where the wild gulls of Devon
Circle wide in mocking wheels,
Diving through the edge of heaven;
Now I know how hell can feel.

And yet there is a part of me,
Still at West Bexington-on-Sea.

Where the furious force-eight tears
And rips at rocks and leaning trees.
I hear her in the battered air
And something in my heart agrees;

There'll always be a part of me,
Here at West Bexington-on-Sea.

THE BELLS OF CHERBOURG

I dreamed the bells of Cherbourg fell
As mellow chestnuts down the years,
While all alone you stood beneath,
Resolve destroyed and clothed in tears.

I felt your melancholy smile,
Your haunted eyes called out to me,
Who for a moment touched your soul -
But nothing more, and fleetingly.

Entwined around the slanting bells
That effortlessly cut through time,
The trials of distance, pain of space,
Mine of yours and yours of mine.

It seems that only we can hear
The scattered peal from summer skies;
The loves, the dreams, the hopes, the fears,
The sad and sacrificial lies.

I dreamed the bells of Cherbourg fell
As light refreshing summer wines,
For just one moment on our world
But endlessly upon our minds.

FROM THE SHORES OF FAR LOCH LOMOND

From the shores of far Loch Lomond,
Over Rowardennan Forest,
Foothills of the Drum of Clashore
Feed the tumbling burns that bind them;
Coursing like the blood of demons
From the dark of Lochard Forest;
Forging like Buchanon Smithy
New-born shapes of infant rivers
Snaking North of young Buchlyvie,
On past Cauldhame, on past Kippen,
Under greying summer heavens.
Gracefully by Church of Scotland,
Nether Gorse and Patrickston,
The sleepy Forth creeps past the high-stacked
Yellow hayfields of Gargunnock.

THERE'S A HOUSE ON ROCK OF AGES .....

Does the Lord think London's ready,
Ripe and oh, so unsuspecting,
For a 'Sodom and Gomorrah',
For an early Armageddon?
Ready for a sudden showdown,
With the braggarts, city moguls,
Making money out of money,
Like the endless ginger beer root.
Crossing swords with gilt-edged pirates,
Trapped in nets of their own making,
Woven by their index fingers
As they make their passage homeward,
Past the orbital and outwards
On to neat mock-tudor houses,
'La Rochelle' and 'San Sebastian',
Each devouring 'M' Reg. Rovers.
Each with waiting wives and children,
All with different conversations,
No one listening to the other,
Over rattling ice-cube tumblers,
Golf Club gifts to gilt-edged pirates.
Cocoa drinkers want a story
As the skin forms on their night-cap -
'Pooh's adventure's' once again please'
Induce dreams with whisky vapours,
Pouring from the gilt-edged pirates.
'That's enough, some more tomorrow',
Little knowing that tomorrow,
Comes the day that's like no other,
Comes the day of final conflict.
Lined on one side gilt-edged pirates,
On the other cocoa drinkers.

On the side of gilt-edged pirates,
In forthcoming Armageddon,
Men of stealth, the gemmy gentry.
Uninvited guests who wander,
Fleet of foot and light of finger,
Through the semis of the suburbs,
Through the rented rooms of flatland,
Past alarms and residential
Porters guarding smart apartments,
Ease the leaded lights of Epsom,
Slip the skylights of Carshalton,
Slide the stained-glass doors of Bromley,
Like boy scouts on Bob-a-job week,
Calling cards from gemmy gentry,
'Job well done' you'll see tomorrow.
Gemmy gentry rise mid-morning,
Greeted by the hookey players,
Off with one excuse or other,
Knowing there will be a handout,
Knowing not just where it came from,
- hookey players don't ask questions.
'Videos of all my favourites,
Yogi Bear and Tom and Jerry',
This one here has some boys name on.
Toys by other families cherished,
Sped by pick-up through the small hours,
By the evil night-time farmers,
Sowing little, reaping plenty.
Scant in love for fellow humans
Save his kind, the gemmy gentry.
Tomorrow sees these rotten apples,
On the side of gilt-edged pirates,
Querying the opposition,
And to them its strange inclusion,
Of the little cocoa drinkers
And their peers, the hookey players.

Gilt-edged pirates and their bedmates,
Gemmy gentry, stand with others
There among their liquor tyrants,
Alcohol-inflamed oppressors,
On a tidal wave of violence,
Sweeping all that's weak before it.
No respect for age or station,
No respect for life of living,
Theirs not to apply the logic,
Any common-sense or reason;
Their's to bulldog, bludgeon, bully,
Quaff the cans of beer and lager,
Alcohol that gives them courage,
Alcohol that dulls the senses,
Foaming head of Armageddon.

His excellence the blind designer,
Foisting all his own shortcomings,
On newly-weds and first-time buyers,
Bland and flat facades and facias,
Unrelieved and unbecoming,
Former glories that surround them,
Dwarfed beneath the lifeless boxes,
Boxes sung about by Seeger,
Grandsons of the standardising.
Sired by austere post-war siblings,
Raised in clean lines by Curbusier,
Sans inherent life or spirit.
Little cares the blind designer,
- doesn't live in his creations.
He inhabits pine-clad parkland
Bordering the fourteenth fairway,
Just a short walk from the clubhouse,
(Doors are closed to all but Creosus,
Vintage 'tablers', blind designers),
Where the bragging mashie swingers
Reap more business than the office,
Deals stand above suspicion -
Where more open than the clubhouse?
How more honest than a handshake

When that hand has shot an eagle?
Contracts made as emblemed sweater,
Tugged, reveals tousled forehead,
Temple thick but slightly greying,
And the knowing smile that binds him,
To the next round of distinction.
No need now for more designing,
Use the architectural standby -
One design will do forever.
Clever? Free to practice putting!
Only this will be the last round.
Dawn will see a different blueprint.

There's a house on rock of ages,.....
One that's not of earthly building;
On which preservation order
Can't be overturned by mortal,
Or recinded by the council,
Nor divided into portions,
For the avaricious schemer.
This house stands against the others
In tomorrows confrontation.
Wall to wall, too wide to measure;
Undefined the elevations,
Different view to each observer.
All except the blind designer.
Too unspeakable in beauty,
Too much soul for him to notice,
That his spiritless creation's,
In the path of ......

Armageddon.

PRAYER

We have nothing that we were not given,
We have no-one who is really our own;
Nowhere to hide that we couldn't be seen
And nothing to fear from being alone.